THE LITTLE BOOK OF

GHOSTS

AND

HAUNTINGS

First published in 2025 by OH
An Imprint of HEADLINE PUBLISHING GROUP LIMITED

1

Disclaimer:

Cataloguing in Publication Data is available from the British Library

ISBN 978-1-03542-292-0

Compiled and written by: Stella Caldwell
Editorial: Saneaah Muhammad
Designed and typset in Warnock Pro by: Tony Seddon
Project manager: Russell Porter
Production: Arlene Lestrade
Printed and bound in Dubai

Headline's policy is to use papers that are natural,
renewable and recyclable products and made from
wood grown in well-managed forests and other
controlled sources. The logging and manufacturing
processes are expected to conform to the
environmental regulations of the country of origin.

HEADLINE PUBLISHING GROUP LIMITED
An Hachette UK Company
Carmelite House, 50 Victoria Embankment, London EC4Y 0DZ

The authorised representative in the EEA is Hachette Ireland, 8 Castlecourt Centre,
Dublin 15, D15 XTP3, Ireland (email: info@hbgi.ie)

www.headline.co.uk www.hachette.co.uk

THE LITTLE BOOK OF
GHOSTS
AND
HAUNTINGS

Tales of the Uncanny

CONTENTS

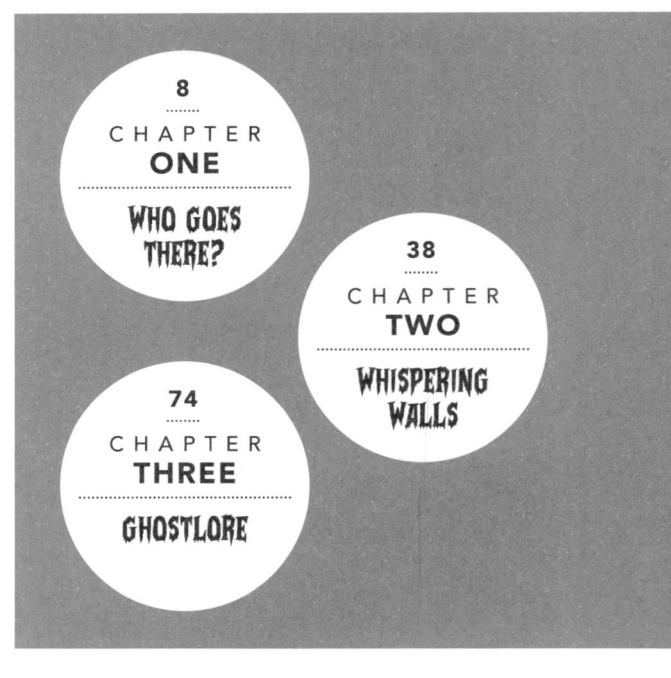

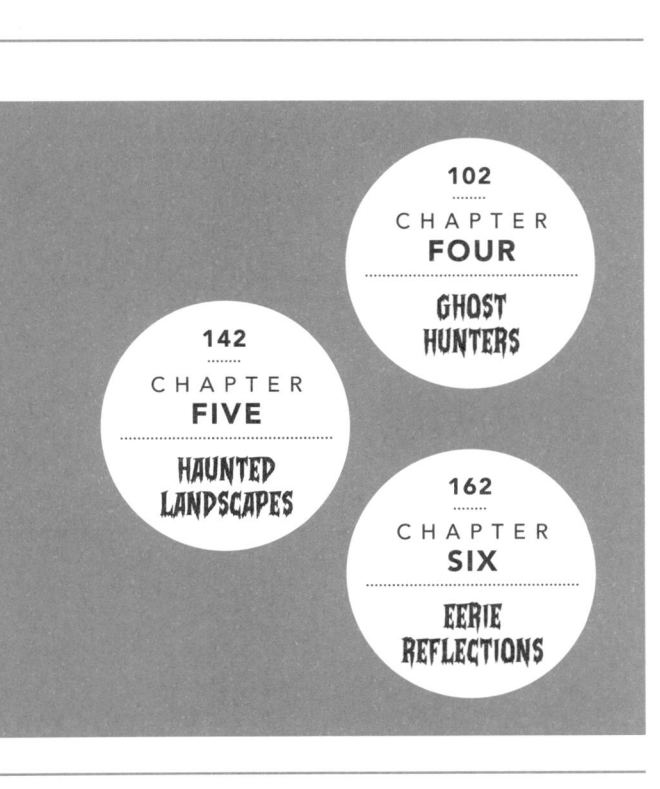

INTRODUCTION

Ghosts have long haunted our imaginations, our stories, our folklore... Flickering at the edges of belief, they taunt us with whispers of the unknown. Are they restless spirits caught between worlds? Echoes of traumatic events, somehow imprinted on time? Or are these phantoms merely the tricks of a frightened mind?

From ancient hauntings to modern-day poltergeists, this little book invites you to delve into the unsettling world of the supernatural. Inside, you'll wander through haunted houses and castles, tread across battlefields echoing with ghostly cries and discover desolate landscapes where the dead linger still. With each turn of the page, prepare to encounter mysteries that blur the line between the seen and the unseen.

Throughout history, ghost hunters, mediums and scientists have attempted to bridge the mysterious divide between the living and the dead. Armed with curiosity, courage and cutting-edge tools and technology, they have attempted to or prove – or disprove – the paranormal.

Discover famous ghost hunters, past and present, and read about some of their most unnerving cases.

It's hardly surprising that ghosts loom large in the world of storytelling, shaping iconic works on page and screen. From Shakespeare's tormented spectres to the unsettling twists in the gothic classic *The Turn of the Screw*, and from the eerie revelations in cinema's *The Sixth Sense* to the comedic chaos of *Ghostbusters*, these unearthly tales reflect our fascination with the unexplained – and our attempts to grapple with what lies beyond the veil of life.

Throughout these pages, you'll find evocative quotes, intriguing facts and spooky snippets of lore gathered from across cultures and centuries. Whether you're a steadfast sceptic or a devoted believer, this book promises to fascinate, to provoke thought – and to send a shiver down your spine.

So, take a step into the shadows – and prepare yourself for a chilling journey into the uncanny.

CHAPTER 1

Who Goes There?

Whispers in the dark, a fleeting shadow, a chilling sense of the unknown… Throughout the ages, ghosts have haunted the human imagination – but what are they?

Are these spectral figures really lost souls, lingering between worlds? Or are they simply tricks of the mind – and mirrors of our deepest fears?

Who Goes There?

The word **ghost** comes from an Old English word, *gāst*, which meant spirit or soul.

The "gh" spelling can be traced back to William Caxton, who brought the printing press to England in the 1470s. He was probably influenced by the Flemish *gheest*.

"

They say that shadows of deceased ghosts
Do haunt the houses and the graves about,
Of such whose life's lamp went untimely out,
Delighting still in their forsaken hosts...

"

Joshua Sylvester
English poet, "They say that shadows of deceased
ghosts", 1595

Who Goes There?

The world's oldest depiction of
a ghost is engraved on a small clay
tablet from Babylon.

Dating back 3,500 years ago,
the ancient tablet – which shows
an elderly male spirit being
guided back to the underworld –
serves as a guide to exorcizing
unwanted spirits.

66
Do not look behind you!
99

Inscribed on an ancient Babylonian tablet, which
served as a guide to exorcism, 1500 BCE

In myth and lore, the witching hour, between 3 am and 4 am, is the time when the boundary between the living and the dead is said to be at its weakest – and when ghosts, witches and other supernatural creatures have their strongest powers.

According to the Bible, Jesus Christ died at 3 pm. That is why the opposite of this time – 3 am – was considered the devil's hour.

66

'Tis the witching hour of night,

Orbed is the moon and bright,

And the stars they glisten, glisten,

Seeming with bright eyes to listen

For what listen they?

99

John Keats
English poet, "A Prophecy: To George Keats
in America", 1818

Who Goes There?

The Roman writer **Pliny the Younger** (61–113 CE) recounted a chilling ghost story in one of his letters. He told of how the philosopher **Athenodorus** – who was staying in an old, abandoned house in Athens – was plagued by the apparition of an old man pulling clanking chains.

When the authorities investigated, they uncovered a buried skeleton bound in chains. After a burial had taken place, the tormented soul was seemingly laid to rest.

66

I am extremely anxious therefore to know whether you believe in the existence of ghosts, and whether they have a real form, and are a sort of divinities, or only the visionary impressions of a terrified imagination.

99

Pliny the Younger
Letter to Lucius Licinius Sura, c. 97–109 CE

Who Goes There?

Curse tablets, thin lead sheets inscribed with spells, have been found across the Roman Empire – often buried in graves or sacred sites.

These inscriptions called on underworld deities and spectral forces to cast curses on people accused of theft, crimes of passion or other misdeeds.

66

May the person who carried off Vilbia from me become liquid as the water. May she who so obscenely devoured her be struck dumb.

99

Inscription etched on a Roman curse tablet discovered at the Roman Baths, Bath, UK (2nd–4th century CE)

With its history of treason, murder and grisly executions, the Tower of London is regarded as one of the most haunted places in the world. Its most famous ghost is the headless figure of Anne Boleyn, the second wife of King Henry VIII. Other spectres include the shadowy figures of the two young princes Edward V and his brother Richard – who are thought to have been murdered in the Tower – and the white silhouette of Lady Jane Grey.

> [My wife looked up] and exclaimed, 'Good God! What is that?' I looked up, and saw a cylindrical figure... hovering between the ceiling and the table... [Then] passing behind my wife, it paused for a moment over her right shoulder... Instantly she crouched down... and shrieked out, 'Oh, Christ! it has seized me!'... Even now, while writing, I feel the fresh horror of that moment.

Edmund Lenthal Swifte

Keeper of the Crown Jewels 1814–52. He claimed his experience took place in the Jewel House (now the Martin Tower) – the "doleful prison" of Anne Boleyn.

Who Goes There?

"

O death! Rock me asleep,
Bring me the quiet rest;
Let pass my weary guiltless ghost
Out of my careful breast.

"

Anne Boleyn
Second wife of Henry VIII, written while she was
imprisoned in the Tower of London, shortly before her
execution on 19 May 1536

66

Life itself is but the
shadow of death, and souls
departed but the shadows
of the living.

99

Thomas Browne
English polymath and author, *The Garden of Cyrus*, 1658

Who Goes There?

"

Millions of spiritual creatures
walk the Earth

Unseen, both when we wake,
and when we sleep…

"

John Milton
English poet and polemicist, *Paradise Lost*, 1667

66

After supper, we fell to talk
of spirits and apparitions,
whereupon many pretty,
particular stories were told, so as
to make me almost afeard
to lie alone...

99

Samuel Pepys
English writer and politician, *Diary of Samuel Pepys*,
23 March 1668

25

North America's first documented haunting took place in Sullivan, Maine, in 1799, when widower Abner Blaisdell and his daughter, Lydia, began hearing ghostly knocks coming from their cellar. Soon, a disembodied voice was telling them she was Nelly Butler — a local woman who had died three years previously.

The haunting, which persisted for months, was apparently witnessed by up to 100 people.

66

I'm the dead wife
of Captain George Butler,
born Nelly Hooper.

99

The ghostly voice allegedly heard by Abner Blaisdell
and his daughter Lydia, 1799

Who Goes There?

❝

O may I join the choir invisible

Of those immortal dead
who live again...

❞

George Eliot
English novelist and poet, "The Choir Invisible", 1867

66

Stars were yet visible, but there was dull light in the east that was not the light of night. The moon had gone down, and a mist crept along the banks of the river, seen through which the trees were the ghosts of trees, and the water was the ghost of water. This earth looked spectral, and so did the pale stars: while the cold eastern glare… might have been likened to the stare of the dead.

99

Charles Dickens
English author, *Our Mutual Friend*, 1865

Who Goes There?

> **"**
>
> It is wonderful that 5,000 years have now elapsed since the creation of the world, and still it is undecided whether or not there has ever been an instance of the spirit of any person appearing after death. All argument is against it; but all belief is for it.
>
> **"**

Samuel Johnson
English writer, from James Boswell, *The Life of Samuel Johnson*, 1791

66

The murdered do haunt their murderers, I believe. I know that ghosts have wandered on earth. Be with me always – take any form – drive me mad! Only do not leave me in this abyss, where I cannot find you!

99

Emily Brontë
English novelist and poet, *Wuthering Heights*, 1847

One of Britain's best-known hauntings is the case of the Epworth Poltergeist. The terrifying events began in December 1716, at Epworth Rectory in Lincolnshire, England – the home of one of the Church's most famous families, the Wesleys.

The phenomena included furniture moving, objects being thrown and inexplicable noises. In January 1717, the events ceased as suddenly as they had started.

"

One night it made such a noise in the
room over our heads, as if several people
were walking then run up and down
stairs... so your father and I rose, and went
down in the dark to light a candle. Just
as we came to the bottom of the broad
stairs... all the bottles under the stairs
(which were many) had been dashed
in a thousand pieces.

"

Susanna Wesley
Writer, theologian and teacher, in a letter to her son
Samuel Wesley Jr, describing the ghostly events at
Epworth Rectory, 1716

Who Goes There?

66

And as to being in a fright,

Allow me to remark

That ghosts have just as good
a right

In every way, to fear the light,

As men to fear the dark.

99

Lewis Carroll
English author and poet, "Phantasmagoria", 1869

66

Death must be so beautiful.
To lie in the soft brown earth,
with the grasses waving above
one's head, and listen to silence.
To have no yesterday, and no
tomorrow. To forget time, to
forgive life, to be at peace.

99

Oscar Wilde
Irish poet and playwright, *The Canterville Ghost*, 1887

Who Goes There?

"

I seriously assure you that I would give 10 years of my life – well, perhaps that offer is rather beyond my means – but when I was a younger man, I would cheerfully have given 10 years of my life to see a ghost – an authentic, indubitable spectre.

"

Thomas Hardy
English novelist and poet, in an interview with
William Archer, 1901

66

Oh whence do you come, my dear friend, to me,
With your golden hair all fallen below your knee,
And your face as white as snowdrops on the lea,
And your voice as hollow as the hollow sea?

From the other world I come back to you:
My locks are uncurled with dripping drenching dew,
You know the old, whilst I know the new:
But to-morrow you shall know this too.

99

Christina Rossetti
"The Poor Ghost", 1904

CHAPTER 2

Whispering Walls

Behind the crumbling walls of ruined castles, within the dusty halls of old mansions, and even in the unassuming rooms of modern homes and hotels, tales of the uncanny persist.

For those who believe, haunted buildings hold more than just history – they are said to shelter the lingering presence of those who never truly left.

Whispering Walls

"

A house is never still in
darkness to those who listen
intently; there is a whispering in
distant chambers, an unearthly
hand presses the snib of the
window, the latch rises. Ghosts
were created when the first man
woke in the night.

"

J. M. Barrie
The Little Minister, 1891

66

Come in, — come in!
and know me better, man!
I am the Ghost of Christmas
Present. Look upon me! You
have never seen the like of
me before!

99

Charles Dickens
A Christmas Carol, 1843

FIVE PHANTOM TYPES

From benevolent spirits to ominous forces, ghosts are said to appear in various forms, each with unique traits. Here are the main types:

Interactive ghost – The most common type of apparition is that of a deceased person. These ghosts may speak, touch you or even emit an odour like tobacco smoke or perfume.

Poltergeist – This word actually means "noisy ghost". From moving objects to slamming doors, poltergeists are usually connected to a particular place and person.

Ecto-mist – If you've ever witnessed an unexplained mist or fog, perhaps it was an ecto-mist. White, grey or even black, these mists are often associated with graveyards and historical sites.

Funnel ghost – This type of ghost may take the form of a swirling funnel, a wisp of light or a swirling spiral of light. It is frequently associated with cold spots.

Orb – This term describes the spherical balls of light that sometimes show up in photos and videos. Sceptics may attribute orbs to dust or other environmental factors, but believers argue they come from beyond the grave...

❝

They're here.

❞

This line from the supernatural horror *Poltergeist* (1982) is considered one of the best movie quotes of all time.

Whispering Walls

"

I have heard it said that as
we keep our birthdays when
we are alive, so the ghosts
of dead people, who are not
easy in their graves, keep the
day they died upon.

"

Charles Dickens
Barnaby Rudge, 1841

"

Gazing down in her white shroud,
Wov'n of windy cloud,
Comes at night the phantom moon;
Comes, and all the shadows soon,
Crowding chambers of the house,
Haunting whispering rooms, arouse; –
Shadows, ghosts, her rays lead on,
Till beneath the cloud
Like a ghost she's gone,
In her gusty shroud,
O'er the haunted house.

"

Madison Cawein
American poet, "The Haunted House", 1896

HORROR HOUSES

With their creaking floors, shadowy hallways and long-hidden secrets, haunted houses are a cornerstone of cinematic horror. Here are four of the best:

The Haunting (1963) – In this classic psychological horror, paranormal investigators take on the sinister Hill House.

The Amityville Horror (1979) – Allegedly based on true events, this film tells the story of a family tormented by spirits in their new home.

The Others (2001) – In this gothic thriller, a mother and her children discover eerie secrets in their isolated mansion.

The Conjuring (2013) – Paranormal investigators help a family terrorized by malevolent forces in their haunted farmhouse.

66

Sometimes the world of the
living gets mixed up with
the world of the dead.

99

Mrs Mills, *The Others*, 2001

Whispering Walls

The Uninvited (1944) is a must-watch for fans of the haunted house genre. This cinematic gem follows siblings Roderick and Pamela Fitzgerald, who buy an abandoned seaside mansion — only to discover it comes with ghostly residents.

Before its release, ghosts in cinema were often played for comedy. *The Univited* was one of the first supernatural films to provide genuine chills and suspense.

66

They call them the haunted shores, these stretches of Devonshire and Cornwall and Ireland which rear up against the westward ocean. Mists gather here... and sea fog... and eerie stories...

99

Roderick Fitzgerald, *The Unvited*, 1944

Whispering Walls

In 1977, strange knockings and other paranormal activity at a north London house placed it at the centre of a media storm. The so-called **Enfield Poltergeist** is now one of the most famous hauntings in history.

The home belonged to the Hodgson family – furniture was said to move on its own, toys were thrown and eerie voices were heard.

Although some investigators believe an elaborate hoax was at play, others remained convinced that the haunting was genuine.

66

[The chair] came off the floor, maybe a half inch I should say, and I saw it slide off to the right about three-and-a-half to four feet before it came to rest. I checked it for hidden wires or any other means by which it could have moved, but there was nothing to explain it.

99

WPC Carolyn Heeps
A police officer called to the Enfield house when paranormal activity was first reported, 1977

Whispering Walls

"

All houses wherein men have lived and died
Are haunted houses. Through the open doors
The harmless phantoms on their errands glide,
With feet that make no sound upon the floors.

We meet them at the doorway, on the stair,
Along the passages they come and go,
Impalpable impressions on the air,
A sense of something moving to and fro.

"

Henry Wadsworth Longfellow
American poet, "Haunted Houses", 1858

66

Yesterday, upon the stair,

I met a man who wasn't there

He wasn't there again today

I wish, I wish he'd go away...

99

William Hughes Mearns
American poet, "Antigonish", 1899.
The poem was inspired by reports of a ghostly figure
roaming the stairs of a house in Antigonish,
Nova Scotia, Canada.

The Winchester Mystery House in San Jose, California, is said to be one of the most haunted places in the US. Sarah Winchester, heiress to the Winchester rifle fortune, bought the eight-room farmhouse in 1886, following the deaths of multiple family members.

By the time of her death, in 1922, the sprawling mansion had 160 rooms, and multiple secret passages and staircases leading nowhere.

Legend has it that Sarah continuously reconstructed the house to confuse the spirits that haunted her.

"

Ten years ago, the handsome residence was apparently ready for occupancy, but improvements and additions are constantly being made, for the reason, it is said, that the owner of the house (Sarah Winchester) believes that when it is entirely completed, she will die. This superstition has resulted in the construction of a maze of domes, turrets, cupolas and towers, covering territory enough for a castle.

"

Article from the *San Jose Daily News*, 29 March, 1895

Whispering Walls

The ghost of **Abraham Lincoln** – the 16th US president, who was assassinated in 1865 – is said to haunt the White House.

Numerous visitors, including Winston Churchill and Queen Wilhelmina of the Netherlands, have reported seeing or sensing Lincoln's presence.

His ghost, often described as solemn and reflective, is most commonly spotted in the Lincoln Bedroom or the Yellow Oval Room.

Good evening, Mr President. You seem to have me at a disadvantage.

Winston Churchill

Reputed words on encountering the ghost of Abraham Lincoln while staying at the White House in 1941. The story goes that Churchill had just emerged from the bath.

Whispering Walls

SIX CREEPY CASTLES

The towering walls and dark passages of castles hold more than history — many are said to harbour restless spirits.

Here are six of the spookiest:

Edinburgh Castle, Scotland – The ghosts of soldiers, a piper and a headless drummer are said to linger here.

Houska Castle, Czech Republic – Built over a large pit in the ground, legend says the castle is a "gateway to hell".

Burg Eltz, Germany – The ghost of Agnes Eltz, who lost her life during a siege, is reported to walk the castle's hallways.

Château de Brissac, France – A woman clothed in a green dress is often seen in the tower room of the chapel.

Leap Castle, Ireland – The "world's most haunted castle" is rumoured to be plagued by a terrifying presence known as "The Elemental".

Bodelwyddan Castle, Wales – Various apparitions, including a soldier and a woman in Victorian dress, have been seen wandering the hallways and staircases.

Whispering Walls

"

Suddenly, two hands were laid on my shoulders. I turned round sharply and saw, as clearly as I see you now, a grey 'Thing', standing a couple of feet from me, with its bent arms raised as if it were cursing me. I cannot describe in words how utterly aweful the 'Thing' was, its very undefinableness rendering the horrible shadow more gruesome.

"

Mildred Darby
Owner of Leap Castle in Roscrea, Ireland,
Occult Review, December 1908

66

I heard one cry in the night, and I heard one laugh afterwards. If I cannot forget that, I shall not be able to sleep again.

99

M. R. James
English author, *Ghost Stories of an Antiquary*, 1904

Have you ever spotted a ghostly face at a window or glimpsed a shadowy figure out of the corner of your eye?

It could be "pareidolia" at play! Psychologists say that our brains are wired to spot familiar shapes – especially faces – in random patterns like mist, light reflections or shadows.

66

Dead people are just like you and me, they still want things. They look at us all the time, and they miss being alive.

99

Peter Straub
American novelist and poet, *The Throat*, 1993

SIX HAUNTED HOTELS

Check into one of these spooky locations, and you might get less sleep than you hoped for!

Toftaholm Herrgård Hotel, Lagan, Sweden – Room 324 is said to be haunted by the ghost of a young man who committed suicide there.

Parador de Jaén, Jaén, Spain – Located in a 13th-century Arab fortress, this hotel is reputed to hide several ghostly secrets.

The Hawthorne Hotel, Salem, Massachusetts – Guests at this spooky venue have reported eerie noises, moving furniture and sightings of a ghostly woman.

Fairmont Empress, Victoria, Canada – The shadowy figure of the hotel's architect, Francis Rattenbury, is often sighted on the lobby staircase.

Ballyseede Castle Hotel, Co. Kerry, Ireland – The ghost of Hilda Blennerhassett, a member of the family who owned the castle, is said to roam the corridors.

The Langham Hotel, London, England – This luxurious hotel reportedly hosts the spirits of a German prince, a Victorian-era doctor and a ghostly figure in military attire.

Whispering Walls

Hinton Ampner, a stately home in Hampshire, England, has long been associated with stories of hauntings.

In the late 18th century, Mary Ricketts wrote a detailed account of "vanishing" figures, slamming doors and chilling cries, which eventually drove the family to flee the house. Rebuilt in the 20th century, the new house has not retained the same reputation for supernatural activity.

It is believed that Hinton Ampner was the inspiration for Henry James' chilling tale *The Turn of the Screw* (1898).

"

I had frequently observed in a favourite cat that was usually in the parlour with me, and when sitting on table or chair with accustomed unconcern she would suddenly slink down as if struck with the greatest terror, conceal herself under my chair, and put her head close to my feet... The servants gave the same account of a spaniel that lived in the house.

"

From the diary of Mary Ricketts, who lived at Hinton Ampner from 1765 until 1772

Glamis Castle, nestled in the Scottish Highlands, is steeped in ghostly lore. Its spectral residents are said to include a mischievous pageboy, a wicked aristocrat and a tongueless woman who has been seen running through the gardens.

The castle's chapel is the haunt of the "Grey Lady", who is believed to be the ghost of Janet Douglas, wife of John, 6th Lord Glamis.

"

I began to consider myself as too far from the living and somewhat too near the dead.

"

Sir Walter Scott
Scottish novelist and poet, after spending a night
at Glamis Castle in 1793

Whispering Walls

Whaley House in San Diego, California, is often called America's most haunted house.

Built on the site of a public execution in 1857, the house was home to the Whaley family — and also served as a theatre and courthouse. Visitors report seeing shadowy figures and hearing footsteps and chilling whispers.

Renowned for its eerie atmosphere, the historic landmark has become a focal point for paranormal enthusiasts and investigations.

The ghostly residents at Whaley House
include:

Yankee Jim Robinson
A thief who was hanged on the land where the
house now stands.

Thomas and Anna Whaley
The original owners of the house, who are
said to appear at the windows.

Violet Whaley
The daughter of Thomas and Anna, who took
her own life, aged 22.

Baby Thomas Jr
The son of Thomas and Anna, who died aged
18 months.

Whispering Walls

Like ancient, drafty castles, old theatres provide the perfect environment for things dark and ghostly. Here are eight haunted performance spaces from around the world:

Theatre Royal Drury Lane

London, England – The "most haunted theatre in the world" is said to be home to multiple spirits, including the "Man in Grey".

Paris Opera House

Paris, France – A mysterious figure in a mask is said to haunt this grand theatre.

Orpheum Theatre

Memphis, Tennessee, US – The phantom of a little girl named Mary reputedly roams the aisles.

Huguang Guild Hall Theatre

Beijing, China – Disembodied voices are rumoured to plague this historic opera house.

Elgin and Winter Garden Theatre,

Toronto, Canada – This 100-year-old theatre is famous for several spooky residents, including ushers who continue their duties from beyond.

Teatro Tapia

San Juan, Puerto Rico – Legend holds that the ghost of an actress who died mid-performance haunts this historic venue.

Palacio de Bellas Artes

Mexico City, Mexico – This stunning cultural hub is believed to host the spirits of performers who once graced its stage.

Theatre Royal

Glasgow, Scotland – The theatre's most famous ghostly resident is "Nora", a cleaner who allegedly jumped to her death.

CHAPTER 3
Ghostlore

From wailing banshees to vengeful spirits, every country has its own ghosts. Shaped by unique beliefs and traditions, these spectres reveal our shared fascination with the mysteries of life and death.

Whether you're a sceptic or a believer, these diverse stories offer a captivating glimpse into different cultures – and draw us into the enigma of what lies beyond…

Ghostlore

66

Whatever its origin, a belief
in spirits seems to have been
common to all the nations of the
ancient world who have left us any
record of themselves. Ghosts began
to walk early, and are walking still,
in spite of the shrill cock-crow of
wir haben ja aufgeklärt ('We have
become enlightened').

99

James Russell Lowell
American poet and critic, *Witchcraft*, 1873

"

Our forefathers looked upon nature with more reverence and horror, before the world was enlightened by learning and philosophy... There was not a village in England that had not a ghost in it, the churchyards were all haunted, every large common had a circle of fairies belonging to it, and there was scarce a shepherd to be met with who had not seen a spirit.

"

Joseph Addison
English poet and playwright, *The Spectator*, 1712

Ghostlore

The Day of the Dead (*Día de los Muertos*), celebrated on 1–2 November, is a lively Mexican festival honouring deceased loved ones.

Families set up altars adorned with photos, marigolds, candles and the favourite foods of the departed. It's believed souls return to visit, guided by these offerings.

In graveyards, people clean tombs, speak to the dead and even sing songs. The atmosphere is celebratory rather than sorrowful – and a reminder that death is a natural part of life.

66

Our feet are planted in
the real world, but we dance
with angels and ghosts.

99

John Cameron Mitchell
American actor, playwright and director

GHOSTS AROUND THE WORLD

From Japan's *yūrei* to Ireland's mournful banshees, each culture weaves unique stories of the afterlife. Here are five spirits from around the world:

Bhoota, Indian – A restless spirit who is prevented from moving on to the next world.

Kuntilanak, Indonesian – The vengeful ghost of a woman who has died in childbirth.

Abiku, Yoruba – A child spirit who torments families.

Dybbuk, Jewish – An evil spirit that clings to the soul of a living person.

Duppy, Caribbean – A malevolent spirit that can cause harm or mischief.

Thailand's ghosts, or *phi*, are deeply rooted in Thai folklore.

One famous story concerns Mae Nak, a devoted wife who tragically died during childbirth while her husband, Mak, was away at war. Unaware of her death, Mak returned home and lived with her ghost.

When Mae Nak's secret was eventually revealed, her spirit turned vengeful and terrorized the village – until eventually, the ghost was trapped in a jar.

Ghostlore

With its torrid history and wild, windswept landscapes, Ireland is steeped in ghostly lore.

Famous legends include the **banshee**, whose chilling wail foretells death; the **Dullahan**, a headless horsemen who rides through the night and is said to be a harbinger of doom; and **Petticoat Loose**, a terrifying figure who appears on lonely, rural roads.

Once a notorious prison,
Kilmainham Gaol in Dublin is
reputedly one of Ireland's most
haunted sites.

The spirits of executed Irish
rebels, including leaders of the
1916 Easter Rising, are said to
roam its echoing corridors.

Ghostlore

"**White Lady**" ghosts are common in many cultures, typically appearing as tragic figures wearing flowing white dresses. They are often linked to sorrowful tales of love, betrayal or loss.

Famous examples include a white lady who is said to haunt the surroundings of **Montmorency Falls** near Quebec City in Canada, and **La Llorona**, a vengeful ghost who haunts bodies of water in Latin America.

Estonia's most famous ghost is a white lady, said to haunt **Haapsalu Castle**.

Legend has it she was a woman who fell in love with a priest. When the pair's relationship was discovered, she was bricked into the castle's walls and left to die.

Many claim that Poveglia, a small, abandoned island located between Venice and Lido in northern Italy, is the world's most haunted place.

During the Black Death, more than 160,000 people were sent there to die, while from 1922, the island housed a mental asylum.

Today Poveglia is off-limits – but illegal visitors report feeling an overwhelming sense of sorrow and of hearing the pitiful cries of the island's lost souls.

66

When an evil man dies, he wakes up in Poveglia.

99

Local saying about the deserted Venetian island of Poveglia

DO YOU BELIEVE?

Do ghosts lurk in the shadows, or are they figments of our imagination?

Across the world, most cultures have some concept of ghosts or spirits – though their interpretations vary widely.

According to recent polls and surveys, the percentage of adults who believe in ghosts (or their possible existence), is:

Malaysia – 57%
Australia – 48%
Canada – 43%
US – 41%
UK – 35%

66

I do not believe in ghosts
but I'm afraid of them.

99

Madame de Staël
French-Swiss philosopher and scholar

Ghostlore

Beneath France's capital lie the **Paris Catacombs**. These extensive underground tunnels house the bones of millions of people, many of whom were moved from overcrowded cemeteries in the late 18th century.

With such a macabre history, the tunnels have become a focus for paranormal lore, with visitors reporting chilling apparitions and inexplicable sounds.

Originally a series of bustling alleyways in Edinburgh, Scotland, **Mary King's Close** was sealed off in the 17th century due to the spread of the plague.

Hidden beneath the Royal Exchange building for centuries, it was rediscovered in the 19th century, and opened to the public in the 2000s.

The close is considered one of Edinburgh's most haunted sites, with reports of strange noises, ghostly apparitions and eerie sensations.

The Monte Cristo Homestead, located in New South Wales, Australia, is said to be the country's most haunted house.

Built in 1885, the mansion's history includes stories of suicide, infidelity and murder. The house is today open to the public, and ghostly apparitions and cold spots are frequently reported.

Chicago's most famous ghost
is **Resurrection Mary**, a 1930s
hitchhiker who haunts the roadside
of Archer Avenue. It's believed the
fashionable blonde was on her way
home from a dance when she was
killed in a hit-and-run accident.

Witnesses report that the ghost,
dressed in a flowing, white dress,
asks for a lift to Resurrection
Cemetery – only to vanish from
the backseat before the destination
is reached.

Ghostlore

"

London is a city of ghosts; you feel them here. Not just of people, but eras. The ghost of Empire, or the blitz, the plague, the smoky ghost of the Great Fire that gave us Christopher Wren's churches and ushered in the Georgian city.

"

A. A. Gill
British journalist and critic, "My London and Welcome to It",
The New York Times, 27 April 2012

> The first thing you notice about New Orleans are the burying grounds – the cemeteries… Going by, you try to be as quiet as possible, better to let them sleep. Greek, Roman, sepulchres-palatial mausoleums made to order… ghosts of women and men who have sinned and who've died and are now living in tombs…

Bob Dylan
American singer-songwriter, *Chronicles, Volume One*, 2004

Ghostlore

The Nigerian tale of **Madam Koi Koi** tells of a former teacher with a penchant for red heels, whose distinctive "koi koi" footsteps echoed as she walked.

The teacher was fired and then later killed in an accident – and legend has it that her vengeful ghost haunts various boarding schools. Students dread the eerie clack of her footsteps as she restlessly paces dark corridors and dormitories.

"

Ghosts

Take shape under moonlight,

materialize in dreams.

Shadows. Silhouettes

of what is no more.

"

Ellen Hopkins
American novelist

In China, corpse walkers were a part of Chinese mourning, particularly in Hunan province. Taoist priests, or "corpse herders", led lines of dead bodies – which were tied together and supported by bamboo poles – back to their hometowns for burial.

These eerie journeys took place at night, with the priests chanting spells. The corpse walkers were welcome at inns because they were said to bring good luck.

66

In Eastern culture, people see ghosts, people talk about ghosts... it's just accepted. And in Western culture it's just not.

99

Jessica Alba
American actress and businesswoman

Ghostlore

Yotsuya Kaidan is one of Japan's most chilling ghost stories.

A tale of murder and revenge, it tells of Oiwa, a loyal wife poisoned and disfigured by her unfaithful husband, Iemon. After her tragic death, Oiwa's vengeful spirit haunts Iemon, driving him to madness and ruin.

Written as a play in 1825, the iconic tale has been adapted for film more than 30 times.

66

I curse you.
You will never be free of me!

99

The vengeful ghost Oiwa torments her unfaithful husband,
Iemon, in the Japanese tale *Yotsuya Kaidan*

CHAPTER 4

Ghost Hunters

From early spiritualists to modern-day ghost hunters, fearless individuals have sought to prove – and disprove – the supernatural.

Armed with everything from rudimentary tools to cutting-edge technology, paranormal investigators look for rational explanations – and seek to bridge the gap between the living and the dead.

Ghost Hunters

"

The boundaries which divide Life from Death are at best shadowy and vague.

"

Edgar Allan Poe
American writer and poet, "The Premature Burial", 1844

66

'Go to the d—l!' said the disappointed ghost hunter... An hour – two – rolled on, and still no spectral visitation; nor did aught intervene to make night hideous; and when the turret-clock sounded at length the hour of three, Ingoldsby, whose patience and grog were alike exhausted, sprang from his chair, saying, 'This is all infernal nonsense, my good fellow. Deuce of any ghost shall we see to-night...'

99

Thomas Ingoldsby
Pseudonym of Richard Barham, English novelist and poet,
The Spectre of Tappington, 1837

Ghost Hunters

The 1800s saw the rapid rise of **spiritualism** – the belief that the dead could communicate with the living.

This movement popularized séances, mediums and other ghost-related practices.

66

Looking back upon my own earliest recollections, I fancy that I was never young, joyous or happy, like other children; my delight was to steal away alone and seek the solitude of woods and fields, but above to wander in churchyards, cathedral cloisters and old monastic ruins... Here strange sounds would ring in my ears, sometimes in the form of exquisite music... sometimes in voices uttering dim prophecies of future events.

99

Emma Hardinge Britten
Advocate for the early English Spiritualist movement,
in her autobiography, 1900

In 1848, two young American sisters from Rochester, New York – Maggie and Kate Fox – claimed spirits were communicating with them through mysterious rapping noises.

Although Maggie eventually admitted they had created the noises by cracking their knuckles and toes, the girls' alleged ability to contact the dead sparked widespread interest in spiritualism – and the pair went on to become famous mediums.

> The ghost not only answers all questions put to it... but the spirit's history of its own affairs is altogether the most marvellous... It states the body it once inhabited was that of a pedlar; that it was 31 years of age and was murdered about four years since by the then occupant of the house... that the first letter of its given name was C, and that of its surname B, but it refused to give the entire name (a very considerate ghost!)

Report from the *Rochester Daily Advertiser* concerning the alleged ability of the Fox sisters to communicate with spirits in their home, May 1848

Ghost Hunters

In 1882, the **Society for Psychical Research** (SPR) was established in London by a group of intellectuals interested in exploring paranormal phenomena with scientific rigour.

Emerging during the height of the Spiritualist movement, its aim was to investigate claims of ghost sightings, mediumship and other unexplained events.

The SPR continues its work today, maintaining archives of psychical research and fostering dialogue between sceptics and believers.

66

The first society to conduct organized scholarly research into human experiences that challenge contemporary scientific models.

99

The stated aim of the Society for Physical Research (SPR)

Ghost Hunters

The first paranormal society in the US – the **American Society for Psychical Research** (ASPR) – was founded in 1885, in Boston, Massachusetts.

Modelled on the UK's Society for Psychical Research, it aimed to scientifically study paranormal phenomena.

Early members included the renowned psychologists William James and G. Stanley Hall.

66

The mystery of death
is not solved by dying just
as the mystery of life is
not solved by living.

99

Henry Sidgwick
First president of the American Society for Psychical
Research (ASPR)

Dowsing rods, originally used for locating water or minerals, became an early ghost-hunting tool.

Ghost hunters used the rods, often L-shaped or Y-shaped, to respond to subtle energy shifts — movements or crossings of the rods were interpreted as signs of paranormal activity.

"

I have been at work for some
time building an apparatus to see
if it is possible for personalities
which have left this earth to
communicate with us.

"

Thomas Edison
American inventor and businessman, in an interview for
The American Magazine, October 1920

Ghost Hunters

The Ghost Club, founded in London in 1862, is one of the world's oldest paranormal organizations.

Early members, such as Charles Dickens and Arthur Conan Doyle, debated spiritualism and mediumship.

In the 1930s, the club explored the famous haunting of Borley Rectory. Today, it investigates sites such as the Tower of London and Edinburgh Castle.

Borley Rectory, built in 1862 in Essex, UK, gained fame as "the most haunted house in England". Paranormal activity included phantom footsteps, ghostly apparitions and mysterious writings on walls. The haunting peaked under Reverend Lionel Foyster in the 1930s, attracting famed ghost hunter Harry Price – a prominent member of the Ghost Club. The rectory burned down in 1939, but its chilling legends endure...

Ghost Hunters

INVESTIGATORS

Hans Holzer – This renowned Austrian-American paranormal researcher is often referred to as the "Father of the Paranormal".

Ed and Lorraine Warren – This US husband-and-wife team founded the New England Society for Psychic Research and investigated numerous high-profile cases, including the Amityville Horror.

Jason Hawes and Grant Wilson – These stars of the TV series *Ghost Hunters* brought the subject into the mainstream.

Zak Bagans – The host of the popular US TV show *Ghost Adventures* has explored haunted locations worldwide, and also owns the Haunted Museum in Las Vegas.

Yvette Fielding – Host of the British TV series *Most Haunted*, Fielding has been called the "First Lady of the Paranormal".

Amy Bruni – A former *Ghost Hunters* investigator and co-host of *Kindred Spirits*, Bruni explores haunted locations with a focus on personal stories.

Harry Price (1881–1948) was a pioneering British paranormal investigator and author. He wrote extensively about his findings, including *The Most Haunted House in England*.

He became famous for his work in both promoting a belief in the paranormal, while also debunking fraudulent mediums and claims.

66

All a sceptic is, is someone who hasn't had an experience yet.

99

Jason Hawes
American paranormal investigator and founder of TAPS
(The Atlantic Paranormal Society)

Ghost Hunters

"

All three of us describe seeing exactly the same thing and that's wonderful because people can't say we imagined it. Many people have seen that ghost, the Man in Grey, but I just saw his bottom half! I couldn't get my head around it. It made me want to investigate more.

"

Yvette Fielding
British paranormal investigator and host of the TV series
Most Haunted, describing a visit to the Theatre Royal Drury Lane
in London, *The Sunday Post*, February 2024

66

Those restless spirits want to be heard. They need to be heard. And those of us who are lucky enough to get to talk to them have a responsibility to listen, really listen, and not just try to treat them like an evening's entertainment.

99

Amy Bruni
American paranormal investigator, *Life with the Afterlife: 13 Truths I Learned about Ghosts*, 2020

Ghost Hunters

66

Do not call up that which
you cannot put down.

99

H. P. Lovecraft
American writer, *The Case of Charles Dexter Ward*, 1941

66

So many ghosts, and
forms of fright,

Have started from their
graves to-night,

They have driven sleep from
mine eyes away:

I will go down to the chapel
and pray.

99

Henry Wadsworth Longfellow
American poet, "Christus: A Mystery", 1893

The First World War significantly influenced the rise of spiritualism, as millions sought solace after the loss of loved ones.

The unprecedented scale of death and the absence of closure for families who couldn't recover their loved ones' remains created a demand for ways to communicate with the deceased.

66

Death is not extinction. Neither the soul nor the body is extinguished or put out of existence. The body weighs just as much as before, the only properties it loses at the moment of death are potential properties. So also, all we can assert concerning the vital principle is that it no longer animates that material organism: we cannot safely make further assertion regarding it, or maintain its activity or its inactivity without further information.

99

Oliver Lodge
English physicist, *Raymond or Life and Death*, 1916.
Lodge was a well-known scientist and pioneer of spiritualism.
After the death of his son Raymond during the First World
War, he claimed to have communicated with him through
mediumship.

Ghost Hunters

Released in 1984, the supernatural film comedy ***Ghostbusters*** – co-written by Dan Aykroyd and Harold Ramis and directed by Ivan Reitman – follows a group of eccentric scientists-turned-ghost hunters battling paranormal threats in New York City.

The film was born out of Aykroyd's lifelong fascination with the paranormal.

> Consciousness survives after death and can be contacted from this world to the next. My family grew up in a legacy. My great-grandfather researched these unexplainable acts. He had his own séance room with a family medium. This is what his family was steeped in. Our family business was a belief in the afterlife and the release of the consciousness.

Dan Aykroyd
Canadian-American actor and screenwriter who co-wrote
Ghostbusters, in an interview with *The Medium*, 2021

Ghost Hunters

"

I ain't 'fraid of no ghost.

"

Ray Parker Jr
Theme tune from *Ghostbusters*, 1984

> 66
>
> I've had some very close encounters with the other side.
>
> 99

Zak Bagans
American paranormal investigator, 2024

Ghost Hunters

Every self-respecting ghost hunter
needs the right kit!
Here are six vital tools:

EMF Meter

(Electromagnetic Field Meter) – Detects
fluctuations in electromagnetic fields, which
some believe could indicate paranormal activity.

Digital Voice Recorder

Used to capture electronic voice phenomena
(EVP), where unexplained voices or sounds are
believed to come from ghosts.

Infrared Thermometer

Measures temperature changes in the
environment. A sudden drop, known as a "cold
spot", is commonly associated with hauntings.

Ghost Box

This device scans radio frequencies rapidly,
purportedly allowing spirits to communicate
through fragmented words or phrases picked up
by the device.

Night Vision Camera

Enables investigators to record in low-light
conditions.

Motion Sensor Lights

Allows ghost hunters to identify unexplained
movement or activity, especially in dark,
isolated locations.

Ghost Hunters

"

They thought of All Hallows'
Night and the billion ghosts
awandering the lonely lanes in cold
winds and strange smokes.

"

Ray Bradbury
American author and screenwriter, *The Halloween Tree*,
1972

66

There are such things as ghosts. People everywhere have always known that. And we believe in them every bit as much as Homer did. Only now, we call them by different names. Memory. The unconscious.

99

Donna Tartt
American novelist, *The Secret History*, 1992

The Ouija board was named in 1890 by an American medium called Helen Peters. The story goes she was using the board with her brother-in-law, Elijah Bond, and asked what they should call it.

The answer "Ouija" was spelled out, a combination of the French and German words for "yes" – "oui" and "ja".

The building where the board was named – in Baltimore, Maryland – is now a 7-11 convenience store. A plaque commemorates the event on the wall.

66

She wasn't religious. She didn't
believe in heaven or hell, only in
ghosts, Ouija boards, tables which
rapped and little inept voices
speaking plaintively of flowers.

99

Graham Greene
English author and journalist, *Brighton Rock*, 1938

Ghost Hunters

PARANORMAL HOTSPOTS

Ready for a spine-tingling adventure?

These destinations are packed with haunted history and spooky chills.

Eastern State Penitentiary

Philadelphia, US – Ghost hunters to this historic prison hope to glimpse ghostly inmates in its abandoned cells.

Aokigahara Forest

Japan – Also known as "Suicide Forest", this eerie location near Mount Fuji is famous for its unsettling atmosphere and reports of paranormal activity.

The Myrtles Plantation

Louisiana, US – Dubbed one of America's most haunted homes, this plantation is associated with numerous ghostly legends.

Fairmont Banff Springs Hotel

Canada – This luxurious hotel in the Canadian Rockies abounds with tales of spectral visitors.

Isla de las Muñecas

Mexico – The "Abandoned Island of the Dead Dolls" is as creepy as it sounds! Apparently, the island's caretaker began hanging the dolls from trees to appease the spirit of a drowned girl.

Skirrid Inn

Abergavenny, Wales – Said to be the most haunted pub in Wales, loud footsteps, slamming doors and eerie voices are said to await ghost hunters.

Borgvattnet

Sweden – Built in 1876, this creepy vicarage has attracted paranormal enthusiasts for decades.

Old Changi Hospital

Singapore – Shadowy figures and eerie sounds are said to haunt this former military hospital.

Ghost Hunters

> ## 66
>
> Maybe all the people who
> say ghosts don't exist are just
> afraid to admit that they do.
>
> ## 99

Michael Ende
German writer, *The Neverending Story*, 1979

66

'We don't believe in ghosts, Mrs Phipps.'

'Don't matter if you believe in them or not. If they're there, they're there.'

99

Joan Lowery Nixon
American author, *The Haunting*, 1998

141

CHAPTER 5

Haunted Landscapes

From desolate moors and shadowy forests
to wild and windswept shores, such settings
are alive with ghostly tales.

Some say the land and sea can absorb
the energy of tragedy and grief, creating a
supernatural imprint. Or do lost souls
truly linger in these haunted places?

Haunted Landscapes

"

The stars were shining, and the leaves rustled in the woods ever so mournful; and I heard an owl, away off, who-whooing about somebody that was dead, and a whippowill and a dog crying about somebody that was going to die; and the wind was trying to whisper something to me and I couldn't make out what it was, and so it made the cold shivers run over me...

...Then away out in the woods
I heard that kind of a sound that a
ghost makes when it wants to tell
about something that's on its mind
and can't make itself understood,
and so can't rest easy in its grave,
and has to go about that way every
night grieving.

"

Mark Twain
American author, *The Adventures of Huckleberry Finn*, 1885

Haunted Landscapes

66

The skies they were ashen and sober;
The leaves they were crispèd and sere –
The leaves they were withering and sere;
It was night in the lonesome October
Of my most immemorial year;
It was hard by the dim lake of Auber,
In the misty mid region of Weir –
It was down by the dank tarn of Auber,
In the ghoul-haunted woodland of Weir.

99

Edgar Allan Poe
American author, "Ulalume", 1847

"

There's always a ship comes into the Clyde
On the grim last night o' the year,
Whatever the wind, whatever the tide,
And whether it's thick or clear.
There's nought can keep her away
from the Clyde
On the grim last night o' the year.

"

John Joy Bell
Scottish journalist, poet and writer, "The Ghost Ship", 1910

Lake Lanier, in Georgia, US, is said to be haunted. Built over a submerged town and cemetery in the 1950s, the spooky lake is linked to unexplained drownings and accidents.

Rumours abound of swimmers being pulled under by ghostly hands and of sightings of the "Lady of the Lake" – said to be the ghost of Delia Parker Young, who went missing after her car plunged into the lake in 1958.

> In New York, near the eastern shore of the Hudson, there is a little valley... which is one of the quietest places in the whole world. This sequestered glen has long been known by the name of SLEEPY HOLLOW. A drowsy, dreamy influence seems to hang over the land, and to pervade the very atmosphere. The place is under the sway of some witching power that holds a spell over the minds of the good people...

Washington Irving
American short story writer, *The Legend of Sleepy Hollow*, 1820

Haunted Landscapes

RESTLESS BATTLEFIELDS

Throughout history, battlefields have seen unimaginable suffering – so it is hardly surprising that these sites are regarded as places where the souls of the fallen linger...

Gettysburg Battlefield

Pennsylvania, US – The bloodiest battle of the American Civil War occurred here in 1863. Visitors report seeing phantom soldiers and hearing gunfire and screams.

Culloden Battlefield

Scotland – Thousands of Highlanders were slaughtered at this 1746 battle. Although it was the last battle fought on British soil, some say the fighting has never stopped...

Passchendaele

Belgium – The village of Passchendaele, the site of one of the First World War's bloodiest battles, is said to be haunted by ghostly gunfire and apparitions.

Chibichiri Cave

Okinawa, Japan – During the 1945 Battle of Okinawa, this cave became a site of immense suffering. Visitors report cold spots and feeling an overwhelming sense of sadness.

Little Big Horn Battlefield

Montana, US – Witnesses report hearing galloping horses and battle cries at this site where General Custer made his last stand, in 1876.

Haunted Landscapes

"

Then the tapping began again, but it was much louder now; and it seemed as if hundreds of drowned hands were feeling the hull and loosening bolts and pulling at hatchways…

"

Alfred Noyes
English poet and short story writer, "The Lusitania Waits",
Walking Shadows: Sea Tales and Others, 1918

"

Ghosts seem harder to please than we are; it is as though they haunted for haunting's sake – much as we relive, brood and smoulder over our pasts.

"

Elizabeth Bowen
Anglo-Irish novelist and short story writer,
"The Supernatural in Fiction", 1952

Haunted Landscapes

66

One disagreeable result of whispering is that it seems to evoke an atmosphere of silence, haunted by the ghosts of sound – strange cracks and tickings, the rustling of garments that have no substance in them, and the tread of dreadful feet that would leave no mark on the sea-sand or the winter snow.

99

Charles Dickens
English author, *Bleak House*, 1853

66

Old perfumes wander back from
fields of clover
Seen in the light of suns that long have set;
Beloved ones, whose earthly toil is over,
Draw near, as if they lived among us yet.

99

Sarah Doudney
English fiction writer and poet, "Between the Lights",
c.1875

HAUNTED FORESTS

With their dense, shadowy atmospheres, forests can be unnerving environments. It's hardly surprising that many are associated with spooky tales…

Black Forest, Germany – This bewitching landscape abounds with creepy legends.

Wychwood Forest, England – Visitors tell of feeling invisible hands touching their shoulders.

Dow Hill Forest, Kurseong, India – Legend tells of a headless boy who wanders amongst the trees.

Old House Woods, Virginia, US – The ghosts of soldiers and pirates reputedly haunt this eerie woodland.

Hoia-Baciu Forest, just outside Cluj-Napoca in Romania, has been called the "world's creepiest forest". It was named after a shepherd who went missing there – along with his flock of 200 sheep – and has a reputation for dancing lights, eerie voices and fleeting apparitions.

One of the most mysterious things about the forest is "The Clearing", a circular patch of land at the centre where nothing grows, and which puzzles soil scientists.

Haunted Landscapes

It is said that the ghostly ***Flying Dutchman*** is doomed to sail the seven seas forever. According to myth, the ship was sailing around the Cape of Good Hope when it was sunk by a ferocious storm.

Over the decades, there have been many recorded sightings of the phantom vessel – including by Prince George of Wales, who later became King George V.

Legend tells that seeing the ship is a harbinger of doom…

> **66**
>
> July 11th. At 4 am, the *Flying Dutchman* crossed our bows. A strange red light as of a phantom ship all aglow, in the midst of which light the masts, spars and sails of a brig 200 yards distant stood out in strong relief as she came up on the port bow... Thirteen persons altogether saw her... At 10.45 am, the ordinary seaman who had this morning reported the *Flying Dutchman* fell from the foretopmast crosstrees on to the topgallant forecastle and was smashed to atoms.
>
> **99**

Prince George of Wales
Later King George V, in a diary entry, 1881

Haunted Landscapes

The Queen Mary, docked in Long Beach, California, is a retired ocean liner famous for its ghostly passengers.

Once a luxury ship and Second World War troop transport, it's now a hotel and paranormal hotspot.

Visitors report seeing a shadowy young girl near the pool, a mysterious lady in white and phantom sailors in the engine room.

FIVE GHOSTLY SHIPS

The Caleuche – This ghostly vessel is said to sail around the island of Chiloé on foggy nights.

HMS Victory – Admiral Nelson's flagship, now at anchor in Portsmouth Harbour, England, is allegedly haunted by the ghost of Nelson himself.

The Lady Lovibond – Legend has it that this ship, which was wrecked off the coast of south-east England, is condemned to sail once every 50 years.

The SS American Victory – Now a museum in Tampoa, Florida, this Second World War merchant ship is reportedly haunted by ghostly voices and footsteps.

The SS Valencia – This ship, which sank off the coast of Vancouver, British Columbia, is still occasionally sighted…

CHAPTER 6

Eerie Reflections

Throughout history, ghosts have stood as a symbol of the unknown. They linger in ancient myths, drift through the pages of chilling literature and terrify us with their menacing presence on screen.

Rooted in cultural lore, ghosts reflect our deepest fears and enduring fascination with life beyond the grave.

Eerie Reflections

SHAKESPEARE'S SPECTRES

The plays of Shakespeare are rich with ghostly apparitions, embodying themes of guilt and revenge. Here are some of the most chilling:

King Hamlet, *Hamlet* – Horatio describes how the appearance of the dead king's ghost turns soldiers Barnardo and Marcellus to "a jelly with the act of fear."

Banquo, *Macbeth* – After he is murdered on Macbeth's orders, it doesn't take long for the general Banquo to rise from the grave...

Julius Caesar, *Julius Caesar* – Caesar's ghost appears to Brutus before the Battle of Philippi, foretelling his defeat and death.

Princes Edward and Richard, *Richard III* – These child ghosts are just two of the 11 spirits that taunt Richard III on the eve of the Battle of Bosworth Field.

66

I am thy father's spirit,

Doomed for a certain term to
walk the night

And for the day confined to
fast in fires,

Till the foul crimes done in
my days of nature

Are burnt and purged away.

99

William Shakespeare
Spoken by the ghost, *Hamlet*, Act 1, Scene 5, 1603

Eerie Reflections

66

Now it is the time of night that the graves, all gaping wide,

Every one lets forth his sprite, in the church-way paths to glide.

99

William Shakespeare
A Midsummer Night's Dream, Act 4, Scene 2, 1600

66

I have heard, but not believed,
the spirits o' th' dead

May walk again. If such thing
be, thy mother

Appeared to me last night,
for ne'er was dream

So like a waking.

99

William Shakespeare
The Winter's Tale, Act 3, Scene 3, 1623

Published in 1706, *A True Relation of the Apparition of One Mrs Veal* is a pamphlet by Daniel Defoe.

Recounting the ghostly visitation of Mrs Veal – who appears to her friend Mrs Bargrave in Canterbury, a day after her death – the account, written as a journalistic report, is often regarded as the first "modern" ghost story.

"

Mrs Bargrave is the person to whom Mrs Veal appeared after her death; she is my intimate friend, and I can avouch for her reputation, for these last fifteen or sixteen years, on my own knowledge; and I can confirm the good character she had from her youth, to the time of my acquaintance.

"

Daniel Defoe
English novelist and journalist, *A True Relation of the Apparition of One Mrs Veal*, 1706

Eerie Reflections

Halloween, or All Hallows' Eve, has its origins in the ancient Celtic festival of Samhain, held on 31 October.

The Celts believed this night marked the boundary between the living and the world of the dead, and to ward off ghosts, they lit bonfires and wore costumes.

Trick-or-treating evolved from a medieval custom known as "souling", where poor people would go door to door on All Hallows' Eve, offering prayers for the dead in exchange for food.

> **"**
>
> Tis the night – the night
>
> Of the grave's delight,
>
> And the warlocks are at their play;
>
> Ye think that without,
>
> The wild winds shout,
>
> But no, it is they – it is they!
>
> **"**

Arthur Cleveland Coxe
American bishop, *Halloween, A Romaunt*, 1847

Eerie Reflections

> ❝
> True love is like ghosts,
> which everyone talks about
> and few have seen.
> ❞

François de La Rochefoucauld
French writer, *Maximes*, 1665

> **❝**
> No ghost was ever seen
> by two pair of eyes.
> **❞**

Thomas Carlyle
Scottish historian and essayist, 1836

In 1929, an article by renowned author M. R. James identified five key features of the English ghost story. They were:

1. The pretence of truth

2. "A pleasing terror"

3. No gratuitous bloodshed

4. No "explanation of the machinery"

5. A setting in "the writer's (and reader's) own day."

"

If any of [my stories] succeed
in causing their readers to feel
pleasantly uncomfortable when
walking along a solitary road
at nightfall, or sitting over a
dying fire in the small hours, my
purpose in writing them will
have been attained.

"

M. R. James
English author, preface to *Ghost Stories
of an Antiquary*, 1904

Eerie Reflections

> **"**
>
> In the Borough especially, there still remain some half-dozen old inns, which have preserved their external features unchanged, and which have escaped alike the rage for public improvement, and the encroachments of private speculation. Great, rambling, queer, old places they are, with galleries, and passages, and staircases, wide enough and antiquated enough, to furnish materials for a hundred ghost stories…
>
> **"**

Charles Dickens
English author, *The Posthumous Papers of the Pickwick Club*, 1837

66

Ye who, passing graves by night,

Glance not to the left nor right,

Lest a spirit should arise,

Cold and white, to freeze your
eyes…

99

James Russell Lowell
American poet and critic, "The Ghost-Seer", 1845

CHILLING READS

The Turn of the Screw, Henry James (1898)
– In this gothic classic, a governess working at
a remote country house is haunted by terrifying
apparitions.

Dark Matter, Michelle Paver (2010) – Set
in the late 1930s, this chilling tale tells of
a group on a year-long Arctic expedition –
who discover they are not alone…

The Woman in Black, Susan Hill (1983) –
A young solicitor encounters a vengeful spirit
while visiting the sinister Eel Marsh House.

A Christmas Carol, Charles Dickens (1843) –
The story of miserly Ebenezer Scrooge, who
is visited by four seasonal ghosts.

Pet Sematary, Stephen King (1983) –
A burial ground's dark power resurrects the
dead, with horrifying consequences.

The Little Stranger, Sarah Waters
(2009) – Unsettling, ghostly occurrences
plague a crumbling English manor and
its residents.

Ghost Story, Peter Straub (1979) – Suffused
with creeping dread, this story tells of a group
of friends who are haunted by a dark secret
from their past.

The Seven Moons of Maali Almeida,
Shehan Karunatilaka (2022) – A dead
photographer navigates the afterlife,
uncovering secrets about love, war and
corruption in Sri Lanka.

Eerie Reflections

❝

I shall never forget the afternoon when first I stumbled upon the half-hidden house of the dead.

❞

H. P. Lovecraft
American writer, "The Tomb", 1917

"

The witching hour, somebody had once whispered to her, was a special moment in the middle of the night when every child and every grown-up was in a deep deep sleep, and all the dark things came out from hiding and had the world all to themselves.

"

Roald Dahl
English author, *The BFG*, 1982

181

Eerie Reflections

> ""
> I don't know who he is, but he's
> burned and he wears a weird
> hat and a red and green sweater,
> really dirty. And he uses these
> knives, like giant fingernails…
> ""

Nancy Thompson, *A Nightmare on Elm Street*, 1984

66

I see dead people.

99

Cole Sear, *The Sixth Sense*, 1999

SPOOKY TV

From spine-chilling investigations to humorous hauntings, there are plenty of creepy shows for paranormal enthusiasts.

Here are six of the best:

The Haunting of Bly Manor (2020) – This atmospheric series is an update of Henry James' gothic masterpiece, *The Turn of the Screw.*

Ghosts US (2019–) – A spinoff of the hugely popular *Ghosts UK*, this quirky sitcom is packed full of comical ghostly characters.

The Enfield Haunting (2015) – Based on the famous London case of 1977, this three-part horror series is packed with scares.

The Haunting of Hill House (2018) – This modern reimagining of Shirley Jackson's novel combines psychological depth with creeping horror.

School Spirits (2023) – Combining dark humour and supernatural twists, this is the tale of a teen ghost investigating her own disappearance.

Lockwood & Co (2023) – This spooky detective series is set in an alternate London plagued by ghosts.

Eerie Reflections

> 66
>
> The more enlightened our houses are, the more their walls ooze ghosts.
>
> 99

Italo Calvino
Italian journalist and writer, in a lecture
delivered in Italy, 1967

66

What's behind the door or
lurking at the top of the stairs
is never as frightening as the
door or the staircase itself.

99

Stephen King
American author, *Danse Macabre*, 1981

Eerie Reflections

66

To be seen is the
ambition of ghosts, and to
be remembered is the
ambition of the dead.

99

Norman O. Brown
American writer, *Love's Body*, 1966

> **"**
> In one aspect, yes, I believe in ghosts, but we create them. We haunt ourselves, and sometimes we do such a good job, we lose track of reality.
> **"**

Laurie Halse Anderson
American writer, *Wintergirls*, 2009

Eerie Reflections

"

Some places speak distinctly.
Certain dank gardens cry aloud
for a murder; certain old houses
demand to be haunted; certain
coasts are set apart for shipwreck.

"

Robert Louis Stevenson
Scottish novelist, essayist and travel writer,
"A Gossip on Romance", 1882

66

Behind every man now alive
stand 30 ghosts, for that is the ratio
by which the dead outnumber
the living.

99

Arthur C. Clarke
English science fiction writer, *2001: A Space Odyssey*,
1968

Eerie Reflections

66

The Supernatural
is the natural,
just not yet understood.

99

Elbert Hubbard
American writer and philosopher